No 628 { All Orders declined unless Postage Stamps are remitted. } SIXPENCE or 12½ Cents.

LACY'S ACTING EDITION.

DICK TURPIN.

THOMAS HAILES LACY,
THEATRICAL BOOKSELLER,
89 STRAND, LONDON; W.C.
(*Opposite Southampton Street, Covent Garden,*)

MITCHELL, 33. Old Bond Street; Roberts, 195, Shoreditch;
BIRMINGHAM, Guest, *Bull Street*; BRISTOL, Bingham,
Broad Street; DUBLIN, Wiseheart, *Suffolk Street*,
EDINBURGH, Sutherland, *Calton Street*; GLASGOW, Love,
Enoch's Square; LEEDS, Ramsden; LIVERPOOL, Meyrick,
Hanover Street; MANCHESTER, Heywood, *Deansgate*; and
Leggett, *Medlock Street, Hulme.*
NEWCASTLE ON TYNE, Allan, *Collingwood Street.*
MELBOURNE, *Australia,* Robertson.

W. V. *Spencer,* 128, Washington Street, BOSTON, U.S.
S. *French,* 122, Nassau Street, NEW YORK.
(BY ORDER) OF ALL BOOKSELLERS IN ENGLAND
THE COLONIES, OR AMERICA,

KNIGHT'S CABINET EDITION OF SHAKSPEARE'S PLAYS, 6D. EACH.

DRAMAS FOR THE DRAWING ROOM, And the Volume for 1859, **PLAYS FOR THE PARLOUR,** } **BY MISS KEATING,** One Shilling each.

ACTING CHARADES by Miss Pickering, 1s.

JOE MILLER'S OWN JEST BOOK. 1s.

Sir E. B. LYTTON'S Plays,

Lady of Lyons—Richelieu—Money—Duchess de la Valliere and Not so Bad as we seem,—In one volume, for 6s. Post Free.

THE LIFE OF A SHOWMAN, Price 1s.

HAZLITT'S ESSAYS ON THE ENGLISH STAGE, 2s. 6d.

READING, SPEAKING AND ACTION, *the Essence of all written upon Elocution, by C. W. Smith, price 4d.*

NO CHARGE FOR POSTAGE.

THE ADVENTURES OF

DICK TURPIN

AND

TOM KING,

A SERIO COMIC DRAMA

IN

TWO ACTS

BY

W. E. SUTER, ESQ

AUTHOR OF

*The Life of an Actress—Dred—Sarah's Young Man—A Quiet
Family—Catherine Howard—A Life's Revenge—The
Felon's Bond, &c. &c.*

———

LONDON :

THOMAS HAILES LACY.

89, STRAND,

(Opposite Southampton Street, Covent Garden Market,)

DICK TURPIN AND TOM KING.

First Performed at Sadlers Wells Theatre.

SQUIRE WATSON, *a decayed gentleman* . Mr. HESLOP.
SQUIRE WHIMSEY, *a rich and gouty justice* Mr. CAMPBELL.
DICK TURPIN } *Knights of the Road* { Mr. PALMER.
TOM KING } { Mr. HONNER.
ADOLPHUS FITZFOOZLE *a cockney on a tour* Mr. J. DUNN.
JACKEY GOOSEGREEN, *a regular chawbacon* Mr. SUTER.
SCOREUM . . . . Mr. GOLDSMITH.

MARY WATSON, *in love with Turpin* . Mrs. WILKINSON.
BETTY SLIMKINS, *a girl that's not to be had* Miss JULIAN.

COSTUMES.

WATSON.—Brown square cut cloth coat, waistcoat, and breeches,
—white stockings, rolled over the knee—square toed shoes with
buckles—white cravat—three cornered hat—white hair.
WHIMSEY.—Claret cloth coat—long white waistcoat—brown
breeches—large shoes, and legs in flannel—bushy black wig.
TURPIN.—Green riding frock, trimmed with gold braid—long
green waistcoat—leather breeches—riding boots—white cravat
—gold laced hat.
KING.—Smock frock over a red riding coat—waistcoat and leather
breeches—riding boots—gold laced hat.
FITZFOOZLE.—Cut off blue coat—light waistcoat and breeches—
light stockings and square toed shoes—three cornered hat.
GOOSBGREFN.—Short smock frock—leather breeches—grey stockings—half boots—red hair.
SCOREUM AND RUSTICS.—Country dresses of the time.

MARY.—Slate coloured silk open gown, with short sleeves, trimmed with lace—white petticoat—ringlets—circular straw hat,
with silk ribbons.
BETTY.—Chintz tuck up dress—apron and circular cap.

PROGRAMME.

VILLAGE OF GREENFIELD.

Tom King amongst the Natives—He obtains a little Private Information, which is not for the Public good—A Robbery not planned but very well executed—A Flat and a Sharp—The Right Time of Day—Discovery but not Conviction—An Unlucky Tourist.

Dick Turpin and his Lady-love.

SQUIRE WHIMSEY'S BREAKFAST PARLOUR.

The Squire boils over, but the Kettle does not—A Female Servant that knows her Place—Jackey is Taken on Trial, and Tries his Master's Temper.

Breakfast for One, but not for the One Intended.

Tom King Visits Squire Whimsey,

And though not well received he yet receives some valuable Tokens of Remembrance.

A Slight Misunderstanding, and a Row in the Building.

THE ROAD !!

Turpin has an Interview with Fitzfoozle, the result of which is agreeable to but one of the parties.

The Tourist has a tale of woe for his Mamma.

First Meeting of TURPIN and KING,

AND A SLIGHT MISUNDERSTANDING.

Dog rob Dog—The Two Highwaymen enter into Partnership—Results hereafter to be specified.

THE VILLAGE !!

The TRUE CHARACTER of TURPIN Discovered.

LOVE AND DESPAIR.

Dick Turpin—3.

A Fond Maiden's Devotion—Arrest of Turpin.

"Many a Slip between the Cup and the Lip."

Fitzfoozle more unfortunate than ever—Tom King is the Right Man in the Right Place—And all's well that ends well.

A ROAD SIDE INN.

FLIGHT OF MARY.

Turpin Resolves on Reformation.

A Stumbling Block in his path—The Bond of Friendship and to what it leads—Mary too has her Resolve, and keeps it.

SQUIRE WHIMSEY'S MANSION.

Jackey visits his Master's Cellar, and if judged by the Company he keeps is a very queer animal—Love making Extraordinary— The Rivals—A little Magic and the Squire turns out to be no Conjurer—A Shake Down and a Rouse Up.

An Attempted Burglary and a Slight Obstacle.

The Robbers in the Wrong Box.

Mary fulfils her Mission—Jackey is a Hero without knowing it— Whimsey is a great Coward and is perfectly aware of it.

KING IS SHOT BY TURPIN.

THE FLIGHT !!

King is staunch to the last, and dies in endeavouring to save his Friend—Whimsey has an unpleasant ride and a very awkward tumble—Jackey gets Promotion.

THE OPEN COUNTRY.

THE HIGHWAYMAN AT BAY.

The Climax of a Woman's Love.

FEARFUL DEATH OF MARY.

CAPTURE & DESPAIR OF TURPIN.

Dick Turpin—4.

DICK TURPIN.

ACT FIRST.

SCENE FIRST.—*Village of Greenfield. Public house,* R., *table with jugs, &c.—benches, &c., at door.*

TOM KING, *in a smock frock*—SCOREUM, JONES, BROWN, *and* VILLAGERS *discovered.—Music lively.*

SCORE. Well, but Master—

TOM. (*with country accent*) John Carter be my name.

SCORE. Well, John Carter, if thee do want work, why don't thee go to the gentry and farmers, and ax for it? It be all very well to sit there, saying funny things, and making us laugh, but that won't earn thee thy bread and cheese.

TOM. Why, you see, Master Scoreum, I ha' been a lucky man in my lifetime—I ha' had good places, and now, though I be out o' work, I bean't distressed, and so I be determined, 'afore I takes another place, to be sartin if it be a downright good 'un.

SCORE. But you be quite a stranger in these parts! What brought you here?

TOM. (*aside*) That you'll learn in good time. (*aloud*) Why, I wur tired of my native place, and so I thought I'd leave it for awhile, and see what the rest of the world wur like—and so I travelled on till I got here, and now as I have already told you, I'd be glad if you'd tell me who are the people well to do in these parts, that I may make my choice among them—who shall have the honour to be my master.

SCORE. Ha, ha, ha! Well, dang it, thee bee'st a conceited sort of a chap, anyhow. Well, I like oddities—I wish, with all my heart, thee may'st get a good place, and settle here, amongst us—thee'd make us merry o' winter nights.

Tom. Ay, would I, Master Scoreum, and prove a good customer to thee—for I know not the lad can drink in a week what I can put out o' sight in a day!

Score. Ecod, I hope you'll come here pretty often!

Tom. (*significantly*) Yes, I'll give you reason to remember my visit, depend upon it. Who are the wealthy people in the neighbourhood?

Score. Why, there be Squire Green, Squire Williams, Squire George Watkins, and a lot more. But I must look after my own business—but if you'll come to me presently, I'll tell you all the people in the place, or near it, who are like to want a strong lad like thee.

Tom. Mind, they must be rich—poor people be no use to me. To be the servant of a rich man is to be of consequence, you know, and I am rather proud in my way. By the bye, who was that gouty old gentleman I saw hobbling past here yesterday?

Score. Oh, Squire Whimsey—and I should think he might suit you very well. He is rich, and I am told he has just discharged his man servant—he's so full of vagaries, and so difficult to please, that nobody stops wi' him long.

Tom. I'll pay my respects to Squire Whimsey in a short time.

Score. There, I can't stop any longer wi' you now—you are as inquisitive as that gentleman who came into the village about four or five weeks ago—he axed me the perticklars of everybody in the neighbourhood.

Tom. Ah! (*aside*) Perhaps one on the same lay. (*aloud*) Indeed! who was he?

Score. Why, he turns out to be a Master Montague; he somehow or other got acquainted with old Squire Watson, who invited him to his house, and there he has remained ever since. Miss Watson, they say, has fallen in love with the gentleman; they are always walking about together—and by all accounts, it is likely to end in a wedding. She is a beautiful and generous girl, and I hope this stranger, if he should be fortunate enough to gain her, may not prove unworthy of the prize.

Tom. (*aside*) Umph! a mere love affair—that's not in my way.

Score. Well, I'm going in to dinner. Come, lads, and do thou come too, and have a bit o' bacon to relish the beer, Mr.— what be thy name again?

Tom. (*rising*) Tom—

Score. Eh?—didn't thee say it wur—

Tom. To be sure I did, John Carter—that wur only a bit o' my fun, one of my jokes. Ha, ha, ha!

SCORE. Oh! he, he, he! Well, thee beest a mortal rum fellow, bean't he lads?

ALL. Yes. He, he, he!

All exeunt into inn, except TOM KING.

TOM. So now I shall be able to commence a very pretty trade—a little rustic indulgence. The metropolis I have made too hot to hold me, and must, therefore, awhile, pursue my professional duties amongst the villagers. In this disguise I can learn the spots where business is to be done; that knowledge gained— Eh, who have we here? (*sits*)

Enter ADOLPHUS FITZFOOZLE, *with portfolio*, L.

FITZ. Well, perforate my pericranium, if this rural tour is not the most extatic preambulatory movement that ever fell to the fortune of Adolphus Fitzfoozle to undertake. Really, this spot is beyond all delightful, and I shall certainly fill my portfolio with its exquisite views.

TOM. (*aside*) A flat! be awake, Tom.

FITZ. Oh, perforate my pericranium! here's a subject for a sketch! A public house, built, no doubt, in the year one, and a regular native in a smock frock sitting before the door. Well, bumpkin!

TOM. Same to you, zur, and many of 'em.

FITZ. Ha, ha, ha! perforate my pericranium! what a perfect idiot! Have I time to sketch this? (*takes out watch*) Oh, yes!

TOM. (*aside*) A gold repeater! just the thing I want for my favourite damsel, blue-eyed Sally.

FITZ. Standing here I have a fine view of the house and the prospect in the distance. Where shall I rest my portfolio? Oh, on this bumpkin's back—I can clap him into the picture afterwards. Bumpkin! come here, you rural idiot—come this way—doesn't the fool hear?

TOM. I ax pardon, I thought you were talking to yourself.

FITZ. Perforate my pericranium! what a savage! Come this way—turn your back. There—(*places portfolio on* TOM'S *back, and prepares to draw*) there, stand still—you shall be rewarded. I don't ask you to do this for nothing.

TOM. (*aside*) I don't intend it.

FITZ. I shall give you something, clodhopper.

TOM. I don't want you to give me anything. (*aside*) I shall take it.

FITZ. Stand still, can't you. (TOM *tries to draw* FITZFOOZLE'S *watch*) It's really impossible that I—stand so. (*places him*) That will do. (TOM *steals his watch*)

Tom. (*aside*) It will so.

Fitz. That's capital—that's the time of day.

Tom. (*aside, looking at watch*) Oh, bless you, I'm no fool, I knows what's o'clock. (*puts up watch, stumbles, and portfolio falls*) Oh, dearee me!

Fitz. Dearee me! (*picks up portfolio*) Perforate my pericranium! if you are not enough to deprive a gentleman of his reason.

Tom. Oh, no! I never takes anything what ain't worth having.

Fitz. I'll have nothing more to do with you. I'll enter the house, and perhaps I may find another bumpkin there not quite so great an idiot as yourself. You're a 'cute fellow to pretend to know what's o'clock. Oh, perforate my pericranium!

Exit into the inn, R.

Tom. Ha, ha, ha! he'll remember (*imitates*) the native in the smock frock. I think I'd better bolt.

Fitzfoozle. (*within*) My watch gone! It is really—that horrid bumpkin has robbed me!

Tom. Discovered his loss already! Ah, it is too late to cut! and so I must play another game! (*pulls off smock frock, and appears in riding coat, breeches, boots, &c.*) I'll stow you away for the present. There—(*hides frock and hat behind house*) and now Tom King's himself again.

Hurried music—Enter, hastily, Scoreum, Brown, Jones, *and* Villagers, *from house,* R.

Fitz. Where is the scoundrel—where is—(*stops on seeing* Tom) Oh, perforate my pericranium!

Tom. (*swaggering*) What is the matter, gentlemen?

Fitz. (*aside*) Eh? this must be somebody of importance! Matter! why, I beg your pardon, sir, but have you seen an ill-looking vagabond lately?

Tom. There is an extremely ugly fellow staring me in the face at the present moment.

Fitz. Indeed! I do not see him!

Tom. You may, with the assistance of a looking glass.

Fitz. Oh, perforate my pericranium!

Score. This gentleman, sir, has been robbed of his gold watch by a fellow in a long smock frock—have you seen such a person?

Tom. Such a fellow as you describe was here not an instant since, and I'm sure cannot be far from you now.

Fitz. Which way did he go?

Tom. Down yonder path.

FITZ. What, the one I see over there to the right?

TOM. No, over the left.

FITZ. Thank'ee, sir—thank'ee—I'll be after him. Come along, friends—I'll reward you. Oh, my gold repeater! What will my mamma say if I lose it? Perforate my pericranium!

Exeunt all but TOM *and* SCOREUM, L.

SCORE. You'll excuse me, sir, but that fellow has diddled me too. I should like to get hold of him, so I mean to try for it.

TOM. Do you?

SCORE. Yes. There's not a soul in my house—you'll excuse the liberty I am taking, but will you have the kindness to take care of it for me?

TOM. Consider—I'm a stranger.

SCORE. Oh, I'm not at all afraid of you—I'm a good judge of physiognomy, and you look like an honest man. *Exit*, L.

TOM. Appearances are often deceptive. It would be a great pity to deceive so confiding a man, so I'll just walk off with all the available property I can lay my hands on, deposit it in some safe place, and then I shall be sure that my worthy landlord cannot be made the prey of those thieving vagabonds who are ever on the look out to trap the unwary.

Music—Exit into the house, R.

SCENE SECOND.—*Front Landscape.*

Enter DICK TURPIN *and* MARY WATSON, L.

MARY. And you love me, Richard?

DICK. Love you! May my mare slip her shoulder, if you are not dearer to me than all else the world can boast.

MARY. Then why not appeal to my father? Why this reserve? We know you only as Richard Montague—you have never said—

DICK. Am I doubted, Mary?

MARY. Oh, no!

DICK. Circumstances, I cannot now reveal, drove me to this village for seclusion—my affairs are in a fair way of adjustment—that accomplished, I think I need not tell my Mary, I should not hesitate to ask her for my wife. By heaven, my heart would bound delightedly could I this instant claim you. Oh, when I think of—

MARY. What, Richard? Why is your manner thus troubled?

DICK. Question me not, Mary. It may be that you will one day loathe as much as now you love me—may curse the very name of—

MARY. What mean you?

DICK. Mary, ere long your doubts, if any, shall be dispelled, the mystery that now enshrouds me dissolved, and when you shall know me for what I really am—

MARY. Richard, you terrify me.

DICK. Nay, be happy, Mary—subdue your curiosity but for a time, and all will yet be well.

MARY. Thanks, dear Richard—you have, indeed, made me happy. My father will rejoice to find you not unworthy—you will forgive him for having doubted you. He is old, and old men are cautious—he loves too devotedly his child, and fears for her sake render him suspicious—but I have never doubted you—never, never, dear Richard.

DICK. (aside) She stabs me to the heart. (to her) Mary, important business calls me from you, I may be absent about a week—but when I do return, all which now perplexes you shall be explained, and then if you reject me—

MARY. Reject you—impossible!

DICK. (dejectedly) Perhaps not, Mary. Return home now —this instant I depart, and till we again meet—

MARY. May heaven bless you, Richard—I will tell my father what you have promised, and he will participate in the joy I feel, and bless, as I shall ever do, the day that brought you to this village, to win the heart of her who would die to make you happy. Farewell—farewell! *Exit*, L.

DICK. Now then, to the road! By heavens, I almost wish some traveller's arm may prove strong enough to conquer— sure enough to destroy me—for at this moment death would be happiness! I must shake off this weakness—I will not turn whimperer! Courage—courage! to the road—to the road! The very sound inspires new life! I am again myself! I am the man for whose head five hundred pounds are offered, and again *he* whom all men fear, bold Dick Turpin, the highwayman.

Music—Exit, R.

———

SCENE THIRD.—*An apartment at Whimsey Hall. Table, chairs, arm chair, stool, and cushion.*

SQUIRE WHIMSEY *discovered at table—breakfast set—crutch —leg bound up with flannel—newspaper and pocket book— snuff box.*

SQUIRE. (*reading newspaper*) "Dreadful robbery! A gentleman on his way home had reached Squash Lane—" Ah, that's a dreadful place! oh, this gout! what a world this is to live in; and as to England, I don't believe there's an honest

man in the nation—we are all rogues—every one of us. Ah !
the country's in a dreadful state ! Betty ! will you come here,
Betty ?

Enter BETTY, L. 1 E.

Do you mean to bring the kettle to-day ?

BETTY. It don't *bile*, sir.

SQUIRE. Don't *bile !* you'll raise my bile, you baggage —get
out of the room. Come here !

BETTY. Lor', sir ! who is to know what you want ?

SQUIRE. Hold your tongue—am I to have any breakfast to-
day ? Why don't you speak ?

BETTY. Why didn't you tell me—

SQUIRE. Hold your tongue ! leave the room this moment.
Oh, this infernal gout ! Where the devil are you going to ?

BETTY. Why there now, if ever—

SQUIRE. Will you be quiet ? what, you want to go, and
leave me to die—to die of gout, grief, and starvation ; but its
just as I say, people will do anything now-a-days—the country's
in a dreadful state.

BETTY. Oh, who would live with a gouty old bachelor ?

SQUIRE. Who wants you to live with a gouty old bachelor ?
Get out of my house this instant—pack up your things and be
off. Come here ! where the devil are you going to ?

BETTY. Didn't you say—

SQUIRE. Hold your tongue ! what a dreadful state my nerves
are in. Come here and tranquillize me.

BETTY. I don't know how, sir.

SQUIRE. Yes you do. Come here and kiss me.

BETTY. What ?

SQUIRE. If you don't kiss me directly, I'll knock you down.
Will you come here ?

BETTY. I can't stop—I must go and make the kettle *bile*.

Exit L.

SQUIRE. There's a pretty sample of a servant for you—won't
kiss her master when she's bid. Oh, the country's in a dreadful state ! I wish I had a man servant. I can't endure that
girl to wait upon me—she excites me so. Oh, this gout !

Enter BETTY, L.

Well, where is the kettle ?

BETTY. It don't *bile* yet.

SQUIRE. Then get out ! come here ! what do you want
with me ?

BETTY. I don't want you.

SQUIRE. Then what did you come for?

BETTY. To tell you that somebody else wants you.

SQUIRE. And who is somebody else?

BETTY. A chap.

SQUIRE. What chap?

BETTY. A chap to look arter the place.

SQUIRE. Oh, what's his name?

BETTY. Jackey—Jacky summat.

SQUIRE. Jackey summat—I don't know anybody of that name. Be off and bring the kettle.

BETTY. It's the chap the woman came to speak about yesterday, his mother, you know.

SQUIRE. Oh, that's the chap, is it, be off and send him in.

BETTY. (*aside*) And a precious queer chap he is—he's fit for nothing, I'm sure, but to look after the pigs. If he comes into the kitchen, I'll dip his head into the *biler*.   *Exit* L. 1 E.

SQUIRE. Now, perhaps, I shall have a little comfort, with a smart, active servant.

Enter JACKY GOOSEGREEN, L. 1 E.

Who the devil are you?

JACKY. Lord bless your stupid head—what doan'tee know I? he, he, he?

SQUIRE. Stupid head! why, you infernal—yet stop—he's rough—so much the better—he's less likely to know anything of the wickedness of the world. Come here, my man.

JACKY. No, no! I ain't your man yet—you're not sure yet that I shall hire you for my master, so it's no use ordering me about.

SQUIRE. Behave yourself, and you will have a good place and an indulgent master. Stand still and don't scratch your head.

JACKY. Why, what hurt can that do you. It ain't your'n! mayn't I do what I like with my own?

SQUIRE. Oh the cub! but I'll endure it, he's simple, and it will be a meritorious action to prevent his falling a prey to the savages that infest mankind. My temper shan't get the better of my philanthropy. What's your name?

JACKY. Jacky Goosegreen.

SQUIRE. Well, then, come here, Greengoose.

JACK. Goosegreen! if you don't know any better than to call a gentleman out of his name, I must teach you.

SQUIRE. Well, that's cool—how the booby stands and stares. I can't bear it. I'm as hot as—

JACKY. Hot, are you? s'pose I open the window.

SQUIRE. Oh, no—oh lord this gout—oh, dear!

JACKY. Gout! what be that? (*lifts his leg—he screams*) I thought that wur an elephant's leg.

SQUIRE. There's ignorance! Go down and fetch the kettle.

JACKY. I hope it biles, 'cos I ain't had any breakfast yet.

SQUIRE. Was there ever such an impudent scoundrel. Oh, the country's in a dreadful state!

JACKY. So I have heard mother say, but I don't care, as long as I have nowt to do and plenty of fat bacon. *Exit* L. 1 E.

SQUIRE. I don't think I can endure it; I'll try—I may make something of him—Yes, I'll try. Oh, this infernal gout!

Enter JACKY, L., *with kettle.*

JACKY. There be the kettle, old chap.

SQUIRE. Old chap! Well, put it down.

JACKY. There, there! (*puts it on ground*) My eye! how hot it is!

SQUIRE. What did you put it down there for?

JACKY. You told me to put it down—how was I to know where? besides, it is so hot that if I hadn't put it down, I must have dropped it.

SQUIRE. Bring it here, you booby.

JACKY. What! do you want me to burn my fingers? No thankee—if you want it come and fetch it.

SQUIRE. Curse you, I can't stir a step.

JACKY. No! well, you bees an old twaddler. Why my brother Tommy, he be only fifteen months old, and he can walk across the room.

SQUIRE. Come and pour some water in here, there's a good fellow.

JACKY. Oh, I don't mind trying, so long as you are civil. (*pours water into teapot, and scalds* SQUIRE'S *hand, who roars out.*

SQUIRE. Oh, oh! take care, you Greengoose.

JACKY. What?

(JACKY'S *attention is called off, and he pours water over* WHIMSEY'S *leg.*

SQUIRE. (*kicking, roaring, and jumping with pain*) Oh, oh! oh, lord! oh you villain!

JACKY. There now, old chap, that will teach you to call me out of my proper name.

SQUIRE. Oh, murder! oh, my leg! Be off! the country's in a dreadful state!

JACKY. You hired I, and I shan't go till I think proper.

SQUIRE. Well, well, I'll endure it a little longer. (*commences breakfast*) Now, tell me, Greengoose—

JACKY. What, do you want me to give you a little more hot water?

SQUIRE. No, no! oh dear!

JACKY. Well, then, be civil.

SQUIRE. Why does your mother wish you to be in service?

JACKY. 'Cos she can't afford to keep me, I am so lazy, and eat so much.

SQUIRE. He's not ashamed to speak the truth—come, I like that! can you run of errands?

JACKY. No, I can't run—I must take my time about everything, particularly my wittals—I be so wery delicate—the least exertion fatigues me.

SQUIRE. Oh, you're a delicate chicken!

JACKY. I believe you. Would you believe it, I be almost ready to drop bringing up that kettle! Well, you are the most ill-mannered chap I ever did see.

SQUIRE. You scoundrel—what do you mean?

JACKY. Why, there you sit stuffing away, and you never so much as say Jacky, have a morsel. I hope you'll know better another time. (*sits at table and begins to eat*)

SQUIRE. You—you—you villain! get up, or I'll knock you down.

JACKY. Be quiet, old chap. If I'm disturbed at my meals. I can't disgust my wittals.

SQUIRE. You disgust me most infernally. Leave the room directly.

JACKY. Oh, if I can't have my breakfast here, I must have it somewhere else. I shouldn't have had no objection to have my breakfast along wi' you, but as you're such disagreeable company, you must wait till I have done.

Takes up tray, and exits, L. 1 E.

SQUIRE. There! come back! get out of my house! Oh, the villain! (*rises—drops into chair*) Oh, this gout! I can't go after him. Oh, lord! the country's in a dreadful state!

Enter TOM KING, *at back,* R. U. E., *and sits in chair* L. *of table,* WHIMSEY *looks up and sees him.*

Who are you? what do you want?

TOM. Really, Mr. Whimsey, your house stands in so secluded a spot—the doors were so delightfully open, and no person in the way, that I could not resist the temptation of walking in.

(*bows with great politeness.*

SQUIRE. Be off, sir! I don't know you.

TOM. Oh, we shall soon be better acquainted. (*sits close to* SQUIRE) Have you any money? but of course you have.

SQUIRE. What if I have any money, fellow?

TOM. Then you'll oblige me by handing it over.

SQUIRE. What do you mean?

TOM. (*presenting pistol*) This will explain!

SQUIRE. Oh, lord! the country's in a dreadful state! Who are you?

TOM. Tom King!

SQUIRE. Oh, murder! take my money. (*gives purse*) Be off! good day! oh, the gout! (*takes snuff from silver box*)

TOM. (*seeing snuff-box*) Would you allow me a pinch? (WHIMSEY *hides box—*TOM *presents pistol—*WHIMSEY *gives it*)

SQUIRE. The country's in a dreadful state!

TOM. I must be going. I have an appointment at *ten*—it must be near the time.

SQUIRE. (*pulling out watch, unconsciously*) It's—
(*sees* TOM *eyeing watch—he hides it quickly.*

TOM. I'll trouble you for that.
(WHIMSEY *refuses—*TOM *presents pistol—*WHIMSEY *gives it.*

SQUIRE. The country's in a dreadful state.

TOM. This will do for a present to my sweetheart. Thank you, sir—thank you—I shall remember your kindness. (*bows*) Good morning—I shall call again to see you.

SQUIRE. You needn't trouble yourself.

TOM. Good morning.

SQUIRE. A precious bad morning for me. (*calls*) Jacky! Jacky!

Enter JACKY, L. 1 E.

Ah! knock him down.

JACKY. I say, old chap, I can't stop here if you make such a row.

SQUIRE. Knock him down, I say.

TOM. To oblige you, with the greatest pleasure. (TOM *knocks* JACKY *down with whip, and crosses to* L.) Good morning, sir. Ha, ha! *Exit,* L.

JACKY. (*on ground*) Oh, lord! oh, lord! I shan't stand this—give me my quarter's wages, and let me go home. (*rises*)

SQUIRE. That was Tom King, the robber.

JACKY. I don't care. What did you tell him to knock me down for?

SQUIRE. I didn't.

JACKY. You did—take that. (*kicks* WHIMSEY'S *gouty foot*)

SQUIRE. Oh, murder! There, you infernal rascal!
(*Music—Hits* JACK *over the head with his crutch—struggle
—table upset—*WHIMSEY *knocked over—row, and closed
in*)

SCENE FOURTH.—*Front Wood.*

Enter FITZFOOZLE, R.

FITZ. Perforate my pericranium! no success. The effort to
discover the clodhopping scoundrel, who purloined my watch,
has entirely failed. My rural tour will not turn out so delightful as I anticipated.

Enter DICK TURPIN, L.

DICK. So, at last. I had almost despaired of booty for to-
day, but am happily deceived in my conjecture. Your servant,
sir. (*bows to* FITZFOOZLE)
FITZ. (*bows*) Sir, your obedient. (*aside*) A very gentlemanly
person. Strolling through the country! An admirer of rural
scenery, probably.
DICK. An idolator, sir.
FITZ. Proud to make your acquaintance, sir. I am myself
an admirer of rurality—on a tour, sir—sketch as I go. Would
you like to look through my portfolio?
DICK. Should feel obliged. (*looking over them*) The drawings
are excellent.
FITZ. You think so? Really you are a person of superior
taste.
DICK. You flatter!
FITZ. If I do, perforate my pericranium. I delight in rural
tours, but have to-day received a sad damp to my enjoyment.
I have been robbed, sir.
DICK. Robbed, sir! you shock and surprise me! What indi-
vidual could be clever enough to—
FITZ. Oh, sir, I blush to say I was the victim of a mere
clodhopper.
DICK. (*aside*) Can there be another professional gentleman
in the neighbourhood? Was it money, sir?
FITZ. No, sir—my watch, sir—a gold repeater. A present
from my mamma, who adores me, sir—how the poor soul will
grieve when she hears of my loss! And to think that I, who
am so exceedingly sharp, should suffer myself to be duped by a
bumpkin.
DICK. Distressing indeed! Your money, then, is in safety?

FITZ. Oh, yes—I have some thirty guineas in my purse, that fortunately escaped.

DICK. I congratulate myself on so fortunate an event.

FITZ. Congratulate *me* you mean.

DICK. No, sir, I congratulate myself—for if you had been robbed of your purse by the bumpkin you mention, it would have deprived me of the pleasure I am about to have in receiving it from you.

FITZ. Oh, perforate my pericranium! what do you mean? I thought you were a gentleman.

DICK. I should be sorry to give the lie to the opinion you have been kind enough to form respecting me—therefore, deliver up your purse this instant, or I shall, in the most genlemanly manner, blow your brains out. (*presents pistol*) I hope I am not rude—my argument is simple and persuasive—but I trust you will not think me wanting in politeness?

FITZ. By no means. I don't admire the conclusion you arrive at—but your arguments are so forcible, that it would be folly for me to say any more on the subject. There, sir. (*gives purse*) Oh, perforate my pericranium! what a delightful tour!

DICK. I shall remember your kindness, Mr.—

FITZ. Adolphus Fitzfoozle, very much at your service, as you are already aware. May I presume to ask the name of so gentlemanly a—(*aside*) cutthroat.

DICK. I am a person of whom you have, doubtless, often heard, and in making whose acquaintance you, of course, feel extreme delight. Sir, I am Dick Turpin.

FITZ. Indeed! (*aside*) If I could now outwit the renowned Dick Turpin, it would be a feat to brag of. I'll try. (*aloud*) Sir, I feel extreme pleasure in being robbed by so justly notorious a—(*aside*) scoundrel. If you would favour me with some slight memento, by which I might prove to my mamma that I have had the honour of meeting you, it would highly gratify me. The pistol you hold in your hand for instance.

DICK. Certainly—take it. (*gives pistol*) And now, sir, I have the honour of wishing you good bye.

FITZ. Stay, you renowned robber, not so fast. I have your pistol, and if you don't instantly restore my purse, if I don't shoot you through the head, perforate my pericranium!

DICK. You won't, I'm sure you won't.

FITZ. If I don't, stifle me! I'll shoot you through the head, if you don't restore my purse instantly.

DICK. You mistake, you won't shoot me, I know you won't, and I'll tell you the reason why you won't.

FITZ. Why?

DICK. Because the pistol happens to be—

FITZ. What, sir?

DICK. Not loaded. Ha, ha, ha!

FITZ. How! (*examines pistol*)

DICK. You'll find it a fact. I never use a loaded pistol with such gentry as yourself. If that pistol had not been harmless you wouldn't have gained possession of it. Dick Turpin is not such a noodle; I can't say as much for Mr. Fitzfoozle! Ha, ha, ha!

FITZ. Here, take it again. (*crosses to* L.) I may be too much for you some day yet. Oh, what will my mamma say—watch, purse! Oh, perforate my pericranium!   *Exit,* L.

DICK. Ha, ha, ha! poor rural tourist! Eh—who have we here? The gentleman I have seen in the village frequently; I hope he has a well-lined purse. (*retires*)

Enter TOM KING, R.

TOM. Eh? that's Mr. Montague, the love making gentleman I saw in the village. I wonder how his purse stands? (*aside*)

DICK. (*advancing*) Servant, sir.

TOM. Sir, your most obedient. (*aside*) He looks warm!

DICK. (*aside*) Signs of opulency!

TOM. Taking a quiet walk, sir?

DICK. Yes, sir. You, I perceive, are similarly indulging.

TOM. Retired spot, sir?

DICK. Very. Good ambush for highwaymen.

TOM. Eh? Yes, I am told there are one or two about.

DICK. I have heard as much. (*aside*) It is idle to waste time. I'll to business. (*takes out pistol*)

TOM. (*aside*) I'll to work at once. (*takes out pistol*)

DICK. } (*presenting pistols, and speaking together*) Your money
TOM. } : or your— Eh?

(*they pause, and look at each other surprised—then burst into a fit of laughter*)

DICK. I'm afraid we are both labouring under a mistake.

TOM. I am afraid so too, sir. Two of a trade, eh?

DICK. Exactly. Your name, pray?

TOM. Tom King. Yours?

DICK. Dick Turpin. Ha, ha, ha!

TOM. What, the celebrated Dick Turpin? Ha, ha, ha!

DICK. What, the renowned Tom King, eh? Ha, ha, ha!

TOM. Delighted to meet you. (*they shake hands*)

DICK. The joy is mutual. I have long wished to see Tom King the notorious.

TOM. And I have been equally anxious to meet Dick Turpin

he renowned—and now, having met, let us be sworn companions.

DICK. Agreed—there's my hand. My friendship for you is sudden, but you will find it lasting.

TOM. And mine, till death terminates it. And it is not unlikely that we may take that bold and last leap together.

DICK. Egad, likely enough. And now to business.

TOM. As you say, to business—and there's likely to be plenty of it hereabouts. Might I presume to advise, we should forsake the road for a short time, and visit a few snug dwellings in the village—there are several. One, Squire Watson's.

DICK. No, no, not there.

TOM. Eh? Oh, I remember, I heard a story of—saw you, indeed, with the old man's pretty daughter this morning.

DICK. I have acted like a villain towards that girl. A highwayman should not pretend to conscience—but when I reflect on what she will endure through me, I curse myself.

TOM. Oh, I perceive. Why, captain, these things will happen to us gentlemen of insinuating address.

DICK. You mistake. She is innocent as when first I saw her. On my arrival at this village, chance threw me in the house of that girl's father—Mary and I were frequently together —she is artless, and I— But why should I enlarge on the matter—she loves me ardently and truly, and I—

TOM. You, I suppose, have been flat enough to return the young lady's passion?

DICK. I love her to madness—what then must I endure to know she can never be mine, to know that in relinquishing her I doom her to misery—endless misery.

TOM. If you like her, why don't you take her?

DICK. No, King, I have promised—sworn to cast aside reserve—and when I shall stand revealed before her—the highwayman, Dick Turpin—she— Oh, will she not then hate and curse me?

TOM. Umph, perhaps not.

DICK. Like a villain, I intended but to ensnare her, and have fallen a victim to my own arts—I am justly punished. One thing I am resolved—I will disclose to her who I am, implore her to forgive me, and bid her adieu for ever. Oh, how could I for a moment think to match with one so lovely and so pure as she.

TOM. Come, come, cheer up—it will end well, I warrant. Let's consult where business may be done. Dick Turpin and Tom King united will prove a terror to all England—and mothers will use our names to quiet their unruly urchins.

Music—Exeunt, L.

SCENE FIFTH.—*Back Wood.   Pretty cottage*, R., *rails, gate, &c.*

Enter WATSON *and* MARY WATSON, L. U. E.

WATSON. Mary, he is worthless I am convinced. There is a recklessness in his manner that can only belong to a depraved mind.

MARY. You are deceived, my father—I am sure you are ; you will find him all that you would wish—a man worthy of the love your daughter has bestowed upon him.

Enter DICK TURPIN, L.

(*running to him*) Ah, Richard ! so soon returned !

DICK. Mr. Watson, I have acted like a villain—gained your daughter's heart, knowing that I could never possess her hand, unless by fraud and treachery.

MARY. Richard !

WATSON. What mean you, sir ?

DICK. Would you consent to wed your daughter to a robber ? Would she consent to be the wife of a notorious highwayman ?

MARY. Surely my senses deceive me—it cannot be ! He cannot be such a wretch—I am not so degraded ! Tell me who you really are.

Enter FITZFOOZLE *suddenly, from house*, R.

FITZ. Dick Turpin ! (*Chord*) I know the gentleman—'tis not long since I had an introduction.

MARY. Can it be ? you are not ! Oh, speak ! you avert your head ! Oh, I am lost—for ever lost !

WATSON. Hence, villain ! No longer pollute this spot with your ruffian presence !

DICK. Mary, forget me—oh, forget me !

MARY. Never—never ! my doom is fixed—'tis misery, despair ! But I forgive you, Richard—may Heaven forgive you also.

DICK. Farewell, Mary. Heaven bless you—farewell for ever.

MARY. Oh, stay, Richard—I have loved, still love you devotedly, were you aught, except—I cannot utter the word. Yet we must not part thus. Father, you will let me speak with him, but for an instant—'tis to take a last farewell.

WATSON. Are you so lost to shame, abandoned girl ? Would you parley with a robber ?

DICK. Yes, dear Mary, we must separate, I will endeavour to become more worthy of you, and then—

MARY. Richard, hear me. It is my fate to love you—I feel

I blush while forced to speak it, I feel that you are dearer to me than my father, than the world! I will never utter a word of reproval to you, I will worship you, through life—let the world shun, persecute you, I will follow you where'er your fate may lead, even to the scaffold. And now, Richard, if you will have me, take me. (*throws herself in his arms*)

DICK. Dear, dear, generous girl! Oh, would I could merit this!

WATSON. Within, there! Lost, abandoned girl!

Enter SCOREUM, BROWN, JONES, *and* SERVANTS, *from house*, R.

WATSON. Bear her away!

DICK. The first who advances will receive a bullet in his head. (*presenting pistol*)

FITZ. Oh, perforate my pericranium!

WATSON. Will you resign my child?

DICK. Yes. Mary, I thank and bless you! I am not worthy of such love—for your father's sake, for your own sake, I ask you—it rends my heart to say it! I implore you, Mary, to forget me!

MARY. Impossible! Oh, Richard—Richard!

(*Music*—MARY *throws her arms round* DICK—SCOREUM, JONES, *and* BROWN *steal round cautiously, and secure him*—FITZFOOZLE *snatches up pistol let fall by* DICK, *and presents pistol at him*—WATSON *drags* MARY *away*.—*Picture*)

FITZ. Now thou art at my mercy, and shall find but very little of it. I told you I should some time prove too much for you.

DICK. That time has not yet come. (*calls*) Hillo! Warhawk! (*to* MEN) Loose your hold, or—

FITZ. (R.) Stir but an inch and I fire!

Enter TOM KING, *hastily*, L. U. E.

TOM. Damme, I'll have first shot!

(TOM *fires, and wounds* FITZFOOZLE *in the arm*—FITZFOOZLE *drops pistol*—DICK *strikes* MEN *who are holding him to the ground*—MARY *runs from her father to* DICK—WATSON *and others advance on* DICK *and* MARY—TOM *defends them with a brace of pistols—they retreat*)

Mizzle, Dick! Back, my pippins! Ha, ha, ha! (*Picture.*)

MEN.

| FITZ. | WATSON. | TOM KING. | MARY AND DICK. |
| R. | | | L. |

END OF ACT FIRST.

ACT SECOND.

SCENE FIRST.—*Interior of a Roadside Inn.*

MARY WATSON *discovered sleeping on a couch*, DICK *standing gazing intently on her—Music slow.*

DICK. Poor girl! exhausted with anxiety and fatigue she sleeps. Oh, what a wretch am I, that have brought such sorrow on her guileless heart, and embittered a life which, but for my destroying presence, would have been one long happy day.

MARY. (*awaking*) Where am I?

DICK. With one whom you should hate, Mary—be advised, return unto your father—'twould break my heart to lose you, but I would, at the expense of life, save you from the degradation you will incur by being the companion of Dick Turpin.

MARY. No, Richard, I have sworn never to quit you. I do not wish to leave—I shall be happy with you, robber though you are—without you existence would be a burthen.

DICK. Your father, Mary?

MARY. Will forgive us, Richard, ere long, I'm sure. I know his kindly heart. Would he but furnish us with the means of flight.

DICK. Would to heaven I could hope it. In a foreign country I might turn to honesty—here I cannot. I am proscribed and hunted—remaining here I know my doom. I may yet for a time evade it, but the day must come when I shall perish on the scaffold.

MARY. Oh, for mercy's sake, Richard, talk not thus?

TOM KING. (*without,* L) Hilloa, there!

MARY. Ah, we are pursued!

DICK. Not so—in this retired spot we are secure from discovery. 'Tis my companion—my friend, Tom King.

Enter TOM KING, L.

TOM. No less a person. Madam, your obedient—you are a bold spirited lass, and I honour you. Dick, my hearty, how fares it with you?

DICK. (*looking on* MARY) Can you ask that question? Yet I fear—

TOM. Pshaw! all will go well, depend on't. Courage—I'll not believe that aught can daunt the bold and fearless Dick Turpin.

DICK. My courage is the same, but—

TOM. Dick, a word. (*aside to him*, L.) There is a gouty old fellow residing in the village yonder, who keeps plenty of cash in the house—I have prepared all for an entry this evening, and so come on, my lad of mettle.

DICK. Tom, hear me. I am not without hope that Mary's father, to lessen the disgrace I have brought upon him and his child, will furnish me with money to quit the kingdom.

TOM. Hope it not, Dick. Report says he is an old skinflint. Rather than wait to ask him for it—make a bold push, and help yourself.

DICK. No, better thoughts have grown within me, and I am resolved to make a strenuous effort to be honest.

TOM. It will fail, depend upon it.

DICK. I pray it may not. At all events, I am determined to wait the old man's answer to my request, and shall not in the mean time plunge into fresh deeds of infamy.

TOM. Infamy! You are, indeed Dick altered, when you can brand our professional duties with so unworthy an epithet.

DICK. Tom, the man who, possessing the affections of a lovely and virtuous girl, would not strive to be himself virtuous, is unworthy the blessing heaven has conferred upon him.

TOM. Well, if lovely woman is to exercise so great an influence on us high-spirited gentlemen, I shall take care to keep out of their reach. Have we not sworn to be companions until death? I will release you from your vow.

DICK. Thanks.

TOM. But not to-night. There is a good booty to be had at old Whimsey's house—I cannot work the dodge alone—you will incur no danger of discovery.

DICK. When did Dick Turpin ever shrink from danger?

TOM. Never! nor would you now did any threaten. Another affair will swell your list no more than a single drop upon the ocean. Come with me to-night, and to-morrow, if you wish it, we separate—I to continue on the road to fortune or the gallows—you to journey leisurely forward on your path to reformation.

DICK. Well, be it so, for to-night, and only to-night, I will be yours. (*to* MARY) Mary, I have business with my friend here demands my absence from you for a short time, and—

MARY. It is not some fresh deed of plunder?

TOM. (*aside*, L.) How knowing these women are!

DICK. No, no, you need not fear, Mary—I shall soon return. In the morning I will see your father, and—

Tom. Come, Dick, there's no time now for the sentimental.
Exit L.

Dick. Farewell, Mary! (*embracing her*) Do not grieve—I shall soon return. Now, now! for my last crime, and henceforth I am an honest man! *Exit after* KING, L.

Mary. His manner was a contradiction to his words. Plunder is their object. Once rid of his companion and—I cannot remain here alone. I will follow him, and should any danger threaten, I may perhaps avert it, or failing that, I'll share it with him.
Exit L.

SCENE SECOND.—*Apartment in Whimsey's House. Window,* R. U. E.—*two candles on table—chairs, &c. &c.*

SQUIRE WHIMSEY *discovered seated at table.*

Squire. The country's in a dreadful state! Oh, this infernal gout! Jacky! Betty! where the devil is that Greengoose? he hasn't been near me for the last hour. This it is to have servants! Oh!

Enter BETTY, L.

Betty. Did you call me, sir?

Squire. Call! I've been bawling till I'm as hoarse as a raven! Where's that fellow?

Betty. What, your new man, sir? he's in the cellar!

Squire. The cellar! what the devil is he doing there?

Betty. Drinking, I think sir. And he's been singing—and when I called out you wanted him, he said you were a gouty old rhinoceros.

Squire The villain! it's no use—I must discharge him. Ah, if I had but a wife? it isn't too late yet! I don't want a rich lady—I want—oh, my toe! Betty, will you have me? don't say no—I'm desperate! I must have a female companion, if it's only a she crocodile.

Betty. (*aside*) I wouldn't have him! I don't like old fogies! I've given my heart to a journeyman tailor.

Enter JACKY, L., *in livery- -tipsy and singing.*

Squire. Silence! why, you're drunk!

Jacky. It ain't my fault if I isn't. I've played the devil with your wine, old chap.

Squire. Oh, the country's in dreadful state!

Jacky. But I didn't like to be so unsociable as to sit drinking in the cellar by myself. I know'd it would be no use to ax you to keep me company, so I took a few bottles under my arm and walked into the pigstye

BETTY. What?

JACKY. It's true, Betty; and I sat down, and the bottle went merrily round, and I and the rest of the pigs were as merry as kittens.

SQUIRE. Why, you didn't give my old port to the pigs.

JACKY. Didn't I though? and if you'd only seen how it made their tails curl— The old sow is as drunk as a hog—and as for the young piggy wiggies, they've rolled into the trough, every one of them as tipsy as lords! they'll have a nice headache in the morning!

SQUIRE. (*throws stick at him*) You vagabond!

JACKY. What, you ain't learnt manners yet? I shall be obliged to lather you again?

SQUIRE. It's no use! I can't stand it any longer! be off— leave my house directly.

JACKY. Why, you ungrateful varmint! is this all my thanks for taking care of you like a *brother?* get some stupid fool to wait on you—you don't deserve a sensible chap like me for a servant.

SQUIRE. Oh, you're as intellectual as a donkey. Give me my stick, Betty, and I'll try and hobble into the next room— I can't stand this fellow.

JACKY. I can hardly stand mysen just now.

SQUIRE. (*aside*) Don't be out of the way, charming Betty— I want to speak to you; but I am afraid of that fellow—he must know nothing about it. Get him out of the way—be near at hand yourself. If I see nothing of this fellow, I'll call " Presto" and you say " Conjorokus," and fly into my arms immediately, will you, eh?

BETTY. Yes, sir! (*aside*) The old fool!

SQUIRE. (*going*) Why don't you come and support me?

JACKY. Support yourself, you're old enough. See how I'm obliged to get my own living.

SQUIRE. Oh you villain! I'll send you off in the morning. Don't you forget, Betty. Oh, this gout! Ah, to think that I should be so afflicted—but nothing surprises me. Oh, the country's in a dreadful state! BETTY *helps him off,* R. *and returns.*

JACKY. Go along, old elephant's legs. (*seizing* BETTY) Betty, don't you think that you and I are two pretty dears.

BETTY. Oh, you fright! I don't want you. Go to your relations!

JACKY. Who be they?

BETTY. The pigs!

JACKY. They're in bed, and I don't like to knock 'em up. Give me a kiss.

BETTY. Let me go, or I'll scream.

JACKY. It's no use. Whenever I have anything to drink I'm always *rumbumtious.*

BETTY. I must try another way. (*looking tenderly at him*) Jacky dear!

JACKY. My eye! why, you ain't been drinking, have you?

BETTY. I'm afraid to stop now, because of Master. I'll come back when all is safe. When he is asleep, I'll cry "Presto," and then you say "Conjorokus"—I shall know it's you.

JACKY. "Presto!" "Conjurokus!" Oh, bless you, my Betty! don't be long, my buttercup and daisy.

BETTY. No, my *artichoke.* Oh, I should like to smother him! *Exit* L., *with one candle.*

JACKY. (*sits*) "Presto!" "Conjurokus!" I hope she won't be long. Yaw! I'm very sleepy! (*tries to blow out candle, but blows on one side several times—when out, lights down*) Capital wine! "conjurokus." I'm as drunk as the pigs! Poor piggies! I must give them some of master's soda water in the morning. Yaw! yaw! old elephant legs. (*lays down in front of table and falls asleep*)

Enter SQUIRE, R.

SQUIRE. Eh? why it's dark! that's not what I bargained for—how the deuce shall I—Betty! Betty, my angel! (*knocks against and upsets chairs*) The devil! oh, my leg!

JACKY. (*wakes*) Eh? why, it's quite dark! When did I come to bed? eh? oh, la! I recollect, I was to meet Betty, and I've been asleep I don't know how many hours, for when I dropped off it was quite light.

SQUIRE. I hear a voice! something stirring—it must be she!

JACKY. There's somebody in the room! Betty, of course!

SQUIRE. (*whispering*) Presto!

JACKY. What's that she says! oh, I know! let's see, what was I to answer—eh? ah! I remember—though I'm drunk, m no fool!

SQUIRE. No answer yet! I'll try again. Presto!

JACKY. Cockolorum jig!

SQUIRE. Cockolorum jig! what does Betty mean by cockolorum jig!

JACKY. (*aside*) Hey! oh, that's wrong! conjurokus—cockolorum jig!

SQUIRE. 'Tis she herself! here, dearest!

JACKY. (*aside*) My eyes, how tender. Where are you, my daffy-down-dilly?

SQUIRE. Here, my rosebud! (*they advance till they bump up against each other*) Oh, my leg!

JACK. Oh, lord, my nose! here, my sweetest. (*puts his arm round* SQUIRE'S *waist*) My wig! she a good armfull!

SQUIRE. (*taking* JACKY'S *hand and kissing it*) Oh, you angel! Whew! how Betty smells of liquor!

JACKY. Why, Betty's making love to me! (*feels* SQUIRE'S *face*) What a strong beard she's got!

SQUIRE. (*kneels with difficulty*) Dear angel, I—curse the gout! why, she's been smoking! oh, the smell of tobacco.

JACKY. Why, she's on her knees! well, I'll plop down too! (*kneels, they throw their arms round each other*) My dearest!

SQUIRE. My angel!

BETTY *enters,* L., *with candles—lights up—*BETTY *laughs—*
SQUIRE *and* JACKY *look at each other in the greatest horror.*

(*throwing* JACKY *away*) The devil!

JACKY. My eyes, if I aren't been making love to an old man with the gout.

SQUIRE. Help me up—help me up!

JACKY. Not I! you got down by yourself, and I'm dished if you mayn't get up by yourself.

BETTY. Dear me, sir, I'm afraid there's some trifling mistake —ha, ha!

SQUIRE. Trifling! well, well, it serves me right—I'm an old fool. For you, Mr. Jacky, I'm ashamed of you. Not content with drinking my wine and getting drunk with the pigs, but you wish to take advantage of an innocent girl.

JACKY. So do you!

SQUIRE. Hem! ah! it's just as I say—the country's in a dreadful state! *Exit* R.

JACKY. Good night, elephant's legs!

BETTY. There—there's a light (*puts candle on table*) for you to get to bed and sleep yourself sober. Let this be a lesson for you. Do you imagine that a young woman like myself, possessing a superior person and address, could fancy a red-headed lout like you? know a little better in future, you ugly cannibal. *Exit* R.

JACKY. I believe you! if I hear anybody cry " Presto" the devil may " Conjurokus" for me, for I won't! Go to bed? not I—it's too much trouble. If the bed would but come to me, I shouldn't mind, but it won't; so I'll lie down and have a snooze here. It'll soon be morning. (*lays down near table, puts cover over him, which throws down candle and puts it out—lights down)* I must put the light out, or master will put me out. I wish I had a bottle of wine here—I'm getting quite sober.

(*sleeps.*

*Music—*TURPIN *and* KING *enter cautiously,* D. F., KING *with a dark lantern, which he opens and looks about.*

TOM. As I told you, nothing can be easier. I know the premises well—the old man sleeps in yonder room. (*points* R. 1 E.) We can avoid that. This is our road for plunder.

(*points* L. 1 E.

DICK. I thought I heard some one breathing.

TOM. The old gentleman snoring, probably. What's this? a candle! very kind of them to leave it, to throw a light upon our operations.

(*lights candle—lights up* TURPIN *stumbles over* JACKY.

DICK. Ha! who's this?

JACKY. (*asleep*) Cockolorum jig!

TOM. Ha, ha, ha! if he wasn't in livery, I should swear it was a drunken conjuror.

JACKY. Betty, you're a deluding vagabond!

TOM. (*passing lantern over* JACKY'S *face*) He's drunk enough. No fear of disturbance from him.

JACKY. (*asleep*) Oh, you thief!

TOM. Eh? (*turns round and puts pistol to* JACKY'S *head*)

DICK. How now?

TOM. I thought the gentleman spoke to me. No—all right —this way!   *Exit* TURPIN *and* KING, L. 1 E.

JACKY. You've got all the clothes, Betty! (*awakes*) Ugh! how cold! such a confounded draught. Eh! a light, and the door open—that accounts for the wind. Oh my—I shall get the lumbago! I'd go to bed, if I warn't too lazy. But how came the door open, and how came the candle to light itself? Eh? oh, lord! (*looks off,* L. 1 E.) There's thieves in the the house. Here's one of them! (*lies down*)

Enter KING, L. 1 E., *with silver and gold goblets, teapots, jugs, &c. &c., which he places on table.*

TOM. There's some of the old man's property, and now for more. This fellow—(*points to* JACKY) Oh, oh! Mr. Cockolorum jig, you'll be surprised when you wake up in the morning!   *Exit* L. 1 E.

JACKY. (*sitting up*) Ta___ a___ Mr. Cockolorum jig does not surprise you *to-night.* I ___ ___ e old master to be robbed, but if I say a word I shall be ___ d and buried in five minutes. (*rises*) But I don't care—master's a good old chap, and I won't stand it. Here! help! murder! thieves! (*calling*)

Music—Enter TOM KING L., *with large bundle—*JACKY *seizes him—*KING *throws him off and throws bundle at him—*JACKY *receives the blow and falls against* WHIMSEY, *who enters,* R. 1 E., *with blanket on—he falls down*

TOM. (*calling off,* L.) Ha, discovered! quick, Dick, bring my pistols, and follow.
(JACKY *gets up and seizes him on one side,* WHIMSEY *on the other.*
JACKY. You shan't go! help! murder!

Enter BETTY, R., *in her bedgown, with a warming pan.*

Lay hold of him—he's a thief! (KING *strives to get clear from* WHIMSEY *and* JACKY.)

Enter DICK, L. 1 E., *with pistol.*

TOM. Fire, Dick, I can't shake them off.
(TURPIN *fires and wounds* KING—WHIMSEY *and* JACKY *fall on their faces—*BETTY *screams and runs off,* L.

Enter MARY, R. U. E.

MARY. Fly, fly! the officers are here.   *Exit* R. U. E.
(TURPIN *follows dragging off* KING, *wounded—a pause—* WHIMSEY *pops up his head and hastily pops it down again.*
SQUIRE. (*sitting up*) Oh, the country's in a dreadful state! poor Jacky! I'm afraid he's killed. Jacky, are you dead? Why don't you answer your master? are you dead?
JACKY. Yes, master! are you? (*they shake hands*)
SQUIRE. Help me up, Jacky. (*they rise*) You're a hero, Jacky.
VOICE. (*outside,* R.) Follow! follow!
JACKY. They're at it! I'll be after them. (*going*)
SQUIRE. Take me with you, Jacky.
JACKY. You must look sharp, then, for I'm going to run, and that's what I never did afore.
SQUIRE. And what I never expect to do again.
JACKY. Come on, old chap. (*drags him by the legs*)
SQUIRE. Don't—oh, my gout! those fellows wanted to rob me, and now you want to murder me. Oh, the country's in a dreadful state!   JACKY *drags him off,* R. U. E.

SCENE THIRD.—*Front Wood. Daybreak.* (*Lights half down.*)

Music—VOICES *outside* R

VOICES. Follow—follow—follow !

Enter MARY, *hastily*, R.

MARY. Oh, Richard! hasten, or we are lost. Fly, for Heaven's sake !

DICK TURPIN *enters*, R. 1 E., *supporting* TOM KING, *who is covered with blood.*

Oh, Richard, you will be captured !

DICK. I cannot help it, Mary. I will not abandon my friend.

KING. Yes, leave me, Dick, it's all up with Tom King—I haven't five minutes' more life in me.

MARY. Richard, you will destroy yourself, but cannot save your friend.

VOICES. (*outside*, R.) This way—to the right—follow !

TOM. There are the bloodhounds ! Away, Dick, 'tis my last request. Good luck attend you. The game is up for me. Cut, Dick, cut !

DICK. (*grasping his hand*) I—I have killed you, Tom—curse on my faithless arm.

TOM. The fortune of war, Dick—better so than—

VOICES. (*outside*, R.) Follow—follow !

KING. They approach ! mizzle, Dick ! Mount Bonny Black Bess and fly. Bless you, old boy—farewell !

DICK. Oh, Tom, farewell for—

TOM. Ever !

MARY. They are here ! come, Richard, away !

Music—MARY *drags* TURPIN *off*, L.

SCOREUM, BROWN, JONES, *and* OFFICERS *enter hastily*, R.— KING *rises and places himself before them, and intercepts them.*

TOM. Stand back ! while one atom of life remains in this carcass, you pass not here. (*endeavouring to call after* TURPIN) Good luck to you, Dick, my boy. Leap, leap Black Bess—stop not for hedge or ditch. Farewell, Dick—farewell the world— it has been a merry one to me ! Stand back, knaves ! I'll bar your passage to the last gasp—to the last—(*falls forward dead*) (*Music—The* CHARACTERS *exeunt*, L. 1 E., *in pursuit*—TWO COUNTRYMEN *carry* TOM *off*, L.

JACKY *enters*, R., *carrying* WHIMSEY *on his back, who has a large broad brimmed hat on.*

JACKY. I can't stand it no longer. (*lets* WHIMSEY *fall*)

SQUIRE. Oh, murder! Jacky, be a good boy, and I'll raise your wages.

JACKY. I ain't had none at all yet.

SQUIRE. You've acted like a hero. You've saved my property—and I'll be a father to you.

JACKY. Will you? then you'll have to marry my mother, and I don't think you'll like that, for she's rather old, and uncommonly ugly.

SQUIRE. You're very much like her, Jacky.

JACKY. If you insult me like that again, I'll jump upon your gouty foot.

SQUIRE. Oh, lord! here, help me up!

JACKY. (*raises him*) There—now get upon my back—make haste, or we shan't be in at the death. Quick—now jump!

SQUIRE. Jump! A fat old gentleman with the gout, jump L. Oh, dear!

(*gets on* JACKY'S *back—business ad lib.—*JACKY *throws him over his head, &c.*)

JACKY. There, now if you don't ride easy, I shall drop you in a ditch.

SQUIRE. (*as* JACKY *is carrying him off*) Oh, lord! the country's in a dreadful state! *Exeunt*, L. 1 E.

SCENE FOURTH.—*Back and Cut Wood.*

Music—Enter DICK TURPIN, L. U. E., *pale and exhausted.*

DICK. 'Tis all over! my pursuers gain upon me. Why should I struggle? why wish to preserve a life which must, from this time forth, be naught but bitterness? Oh, fool—villain that I am, but for this last crime there might have been perhaps in store for me days of peace and happiness, but now—

Music—Enter WATSON, SCOREUM, BROWN, JONES, *and others, hastily*, L. U. E.

WATSON. Surrender—you are unarmed! surrender!

DICK. Were I not unarmed, nor you, nor they, nor any of you would dare to stand before me, and demand that I should yield.

WATSON. Villain, thou hast brought disgrace upon an old man's head—destruction on an innocent and confiding female.

DICK. I know and feel it—your words cannot add one pang to those which now are torturing me to madness.

WATSON. Yield, or we fire.

DICK. Fire, I shall not shrink. Think you I fear death? No, I covet it—let me die now by your hands, and spare you the additional disgrace of knowing that the man your daughter loves must perish on a scaffold.

WATSON. Will you yield?

DICK. No.

WATSON. (*to* MEN) Prepare! Again I ask you, will you yield?

DICK. (*folding his arms determinedly*) With my life only.

WATSON. Yield, or instant death!

MARY. (*without*, L. U. E.) Oh, save him! save him!

WATSON. Fire!

Music—MARY *rushes in*, L. U. E.—*at the instaut they fire, and is shot by them.*

MARY. (*entering*) Father, spare him! Oh!

(TURPIN *utters a cry of horror, and catches her in his arms—* WATSON *runs to her*)

DICK. Mary, Mary! Wretch—monster that I am! 'tis I have slain her!

MARY. Richard, farewell! I have loved—I die for you! Oh, would my death might save you! Father, forgive me! Richard, bless you—bless—ah! (*Music*—MARY *dies*)

DICK. Has no one a pistol for this breast? Why do you not drag me to the scaffold? To live one moment now, is worse than twenty deaths. Heaven's curse is upon me! My own hand destroyed my friend—and now for me this girl dies—dear, devoted Mary! I cannot bear it—madness is upon me! Is there no weapon? To the scaffold! Ah, my knife! (*takes knife from his pocket, and is about to stab himself, when he is seized, and disarmed—he struggles*) Fiends, loose your hold! I know that I am yours—I know that I must linger on for days ere death will come to my relief—I know a felon's doom awaits me! I wish not to escape it, but I will hold once more within my arms her who—(*breaks from them*) Mary—ha, ha, ha! my own loved girl! ha, ha, ha!

(*Music*—He laughs hysterically, and throws himself beside her WATSON *is buried in grief—Picture and*)

R.   L.

CURTAIN.

www.ingramcontent.com/pod-product-compliance
Lightning Source LLC
Chambersburg PA
CBHW081307040426
42452CB00014B/2691